MUNICIPAL SHARED SERVICE AND CONSOLIDATION HANDBOOK

A Practical Guide to a Complex Challenge

MUNICIPAL SHARED SERVICE AND CONSOLIDATION HANDBOOK

A Practical Guide to a Complex Challenge

Edmund M. Henschel

MAVEN MARK BOOKS

Milwaukee, Wisconsin

Published by
MavenMark Books
(an imprint of HenschelHAUS Publishing, Inc.)
www.henschelHAUSbooks.com
Email: info@henschelHAUSbooks.com

Please contact the publisher for inquiries regarding
quantity and academic discounts.

ISBN: 978159598-714-3
E-ISBN: 978159598-715-0
LCCN: 2019901142

*This book is dedicated to my wife, Sherry,
and my children, Greg, Mark, and Victoria,
who all tolerated my long hours and many night
meetings while providing public service
to my communities.*

*"Collaboration is an unnatural act between
non-consenting adults. We all say we want to
collaborate, but what we really mean is that we want
to continue doing things as we have always done them
while others change to fit what we are doing."*
—Former Surgeon General Jocelyn Elders

TABLE OF CONTENTS

ACKNOWLEDGMENTS

This book would not be possible without the encouragement and assistance of a number of people. Dr. John Luthy, President of the Futures Corporation first encouraged me to write this book and share my knowledge and experiences after having served many years as a local government municipal manager.

In addition, several of my students who took my graduate course in local government management offered a number of edits, changes, and improvements to the original manuscript. These students included Gina Vlach, Morgan Aschenbrenner, Mathew Donrath, Jack Johnston, Nancy Garcia, Rachel Hegland, and Chee Herr. I am very grateful to the assistance and knowledge these individuals provided to make this book as meaningful as possible.

I would also like to thank Lesley DeMartini for her support and editorial contributions.

FOREWORD

Always a teacher; always a student. This handbook reflects the author's journey through his professional career. He was well prepared by education and, equally important, by aptitude. He could handle complicated numbers and spread sheets, but he could also clearly and concisely explain them to any internal or external group of administrators or elected officials.

This handbook reflects all that experience and expertise. It addresses the complexities of solving fiscal needs on all local government levels. It could be compared to unwinding a ball of yarn which can be done successfully once one knows where to begin. Similarly putting together the puzzle of combining services only works when one knows where to begin. This book identifies how to do that.

This guide identifies the causes that create the need to collaborate and combine local government operations and services. It often begins with money, tax revenues, rising personnel and/or supply costs, changes in population, etc. The rapid change in technology makes today's operations, service delivery and costs so different from yesterday as the author illustrates.

About the time a reader feels mired in detail and "the tangled yarn" of shared service processes, an example is provided that shines the light of understanding for the reader. Lists are helpful on first reading and remain valuable as the real world is confronted.

This handbook is a worthwhile learning tool for new, as well as seasoned public officials, whether elected or appointed.

Subsequently, the "puzzle pieces" should be on the desks of all individuals involved in public policy to help them untangle the yarn in years to come.

Margaret Farrow
Former Village President
Former Wisconsin Lieutenant Governor

PROLOGUE

I was about a year and a half into my career as a city administrator in a small Michigan suburban city in 1975. It was a middle-class bedroom community where a majority of its residents were employed in the auto industry; a time when cars were selling, people prospered economically, and citizens paid their taxes. When the economy crashed, cars did not sell. People got laid off and many residents became delinquent in paying their property taxes. Cities in Michigan, like in many states, rely heavily on property taxes as a main source of revenue.

A severe recession hit the country from 1975 to 1976. As the economy dipped, so did car sales. This resulted in layoffs in the auto industry, which in turn led to a significant increase in delinquent property taxes and a huge cash flow challenge for my city. While this financial challenge cast a dark cloud over the city, it ultimately presented a silver lining that led to tremendous opportunity.

This book will explore the challenges of shared municipal services and consolidations. It is often necessary for the stars to align in order to create opportunities and to achieve success. In this case, it was my good fortune to have had a very positive relationship with the board chairman of the adjoining township. (Bear in mind that cities and towns don't typically get along very well.) The town had a contract with the county sheriff's department to provide police services, but it was becoming increasingly dissatisfied with the cost of the contract in relation to the services being provided.

My city had a small police department that was inefficient due to its size. The city was surrounded by the town, which meant that sheriff patrol cars regularly went through the city during normal patrols or to respond to calls. This seemed like a duplication of effort. The town board chairman and I, after several meetings, determined that there was an opportunity to save tax dollars, improve service and become more efficient if we created a joint police department and shared the expenses.

It took a lot of meetings, hours of time and a leap of faith by both municipalities to create a joint police department. This effort was supported with the award of a federal demonstration grant. The result was a better police department that provided better service at a reduced cost to both municipalities.

That was my first involvement with shared services, and I have been a strong proponent ever since.

While shared services have proven to be cost effective, improve efficiency and enhance performance, it remains a difficult option for local governments. If it were easy, many more municipalities would be using this approach to provide municipal services. The intent of this book is to guide participants through the frequent challenges, provide a road map to solutions, and enable government leaders to consider the opportunities available within their organizations— whether a city, village, town, school district or not-for-profit organization—to maximize the use of ever scarcer tax dollars.

As government professionals,
we owe it to the taxpayers!

CHAPTER 1
SHARED SERVICES DEFINED

"There is something about building up a comradeship—that I still believe is the greatest of all feats—and sharing in the dangers with your company of peers. It's the intense effort, the giving of everything you've got. It's really a very pleasant sensation."
—Sir Edmund Hillary

Today's structure of local government is a result of the early beginnings of an agrarian society and is based primarily on the structure of government as found in Old England. The States were formed as the central organizational structure of society in the early days, and functions that crossed state lines were relegated to the federal government by the Constitution (and subsequently by interpretation of the courts). The states also relegated various day-to-day administrative functions to local governments (i.e., counties, cities, villages and towns).

Cities developed as both economic and social centers and the location of structured government services. These local units of government became the focal point of governmental services as well as the point of pride and location for the individual psyche. This pride in location is much like how many people identify with and support their local sports teams.

As a result of this identification with place, changing the place becomes difficult. While society has evolved from a primarily agrarian society to one of complex urban and ex-urban areas (to the point that the current geographic boundaries of counties, cities, villages and towns no longer seem logical), boundaries are often found to be inefficient and can promote urban sprawl at a great cost to the taxpayers—yet we do not change them.

As a result, the consolidation or elimination of units of government in modern times has had a nearly failed history in our country with a few exceptions. Thus, the United States functions with over 38,000 units of government based on a system, developed in England centuries ago, that is supposed to efficiently provide government services in a modern world. This makes no sense, but it continues!

Most states impose strict limitations on what local units of government can do, what laws (ordinances) they can pass, and most importantly, how they can finance their various functions and services. The result of these limitations by the states is an atmosphere of competition rather than cooperation. They compete with each other for new businesses for the purpose of a broader and more robust tax base. They compete with each other to have the lowest perceived taxes and the best schools. They compete with each other to hire the best professional staffs. Little effort is put into stepping back, taking a look at the big picture and asking how we can provide our services better, faster and cheaper in a modern age. Is there a better way?

The fact that municipal consolidations (i.e., the joining of two or more municipalities into a single new entity) has had such a dismal track record that this focus is largely ignored in this book. The focus here is on the sharing of specific services between or within a municipality as well as the use of outside resources (outsourcing) in order to save money and create greater efficiency in providing municipal services.

With nearly six billion people in cities worldwide having an on-demand desire for services and a suspicion that all governments are wasteful and inefficient, business as usual is not sustainable. Something must give, and it needs to start at the municipal level—which still has the greatest degree of trust among the citizenry.

So what do we mean by the term "shared services?" One definition of shared services is as follows:

*A **shared service** is the provision of a service by one part of an organization or group where that service had previously been found in more than one part of the organization or group. Thus, the funding and resourcing of the service is shared, and the providing department effectively becomes an internal service provider. The key here is the idea of 'sharing' within an organization or group. This sharing needs to fundamentally include shared accountability of results by the unit from where the work is migrated to the provider. The provider, on the other hand, needs to ensure that the agreed-upon results are delivered based on defined measures.*

A shared service is more than just centralization or consolidation of similar activities in one location. It is the convergence and streamlining of similar functions within an organization, or across organizations, to ensure that they are delivered as effectively and efficiently as possible. In a shared service model, these activities will be run like a business, delivering services to internal and external customers at a cost, quality and timeliness that is competitive with alternatives.

In some spheres, the term "shared services" often carries too much baggage and is too inflammatory to even allow the beginning of meaningful conversations.

Perhaps other terminology should be used in these cases, such as "collaborative transformation." If this is too academic, perhaps they should be referred to as simply "new, better, lower cost ways of working together."

If indeed shared services are "new, better, lower cost way of working together," why do we not do more of it? Consider the following scenario:

When a Midwest mayor recently had a heart attack, he was grateful for the quick response time of the paramedics. After his recovery and return to work, he was talking to his fire chief and noted that he did not recognize the ambulance team that took him to the hospital. The fire chief responded that their ambulance was busy on another call and that he was transported by an ambulance from a neighboring city with whom they had a mutual backup agreement.

The mayor admitted that at the time, the name on the side of the ambulance was irrelevant to him. What was important was a speedy response and receiving the appropriate treatment that resulted in his full recovery.

Similar to the mayor above, most residents care very little about who is providing almost any service. What is important to most is getting high quality service, when it is needed, at the best possible value. So then what's the problem? In most cases, it's the internal organization, the local citizenry (that pride thing) or even elected officials.

Few municipalities have ever had all the money they need to do all the things they desire in the manner that would be most beneficial to its residents/customers. The economic downturn of 2008 made financial resources even scarcer, as property values dropped and there was increased political pressure to avoid tax increases. The fiscal environment facing local governments at that time was surely going to force them to transform the way they were doing business. After all, the fiscal pressures were coming from all directions:

- Less funding from the state and federal governments as they dealt with their own fiscal constraints, resulting in a severe "trickle down" erosion of funding;

- The constraint of local revenue sources due to the economic slow-down, state-imposed revenue/spending caps, and public opposition to any increases in current taxes or the creation of new taxes and fees;

- Continued demand by citizens for a high level of services, even in the face of reduced revenues and increased costs;

- More recently, the desire to limit what government does and to make it "smaller."

1. SHARED SERVICES DEFINED

Many predicted (myself included) that the stars had finally aligned and that the 2008 recession would be the catalyst to foster and encourage shared services—that taxpayers would finally demand it, and elected officials would insist on it.

Unfortunately, what happened as funds got tighter was not a search for ways to provide services faster, cheaper and more efficiently. Instead, municipalities reduced services, froze salaries, limited benefits and created "furlough days." None of this had a significant long-term impact on costs; it was simply a knee-jerk reaction to the immediate shortage of cash. It was as though municipalities were focused on the next quarter's profit projections like corporations do—but municipalities don't operate on profit projections. They are not in the business of making their stockholders rich. Lost by appointed and elected officials is the concept of being the sacred trustees of the tax dollars provided by residents in order to conduct the public's business.

It's time that local government leadership wakes up to the real challenges they are facing. Since the devastating 2008 economic collapse, the economy has rebounded. Property values are slowly increasing, but they are still years away from 2006 values. The state and federal governments are focused on less government, not more, and will not be a source of significant financial assistance in the near term. Restrictive property tax and current local revenue policies cannot survive forever. Hardworking municipal employees cannot continue living with wage freezes and furlough days. The best and the brightest of them will seek employment elsewhere. Accordingly, municipal leaders must be proactive in balancing the ever-changing need to maintain services while limiting tax increases. Failure to do so will inevitably result in elected and appointed officials facing the wrath of constituents at council meetings, on the street and at polling booths across the country.

Many municipalities have already recognized the need to do more—and to do it better, faster and cheaper. Many have looked to shared service arrangements in an ongoing effort to reduce or stabilize costs

Figure 1: The Shared Services Continuum

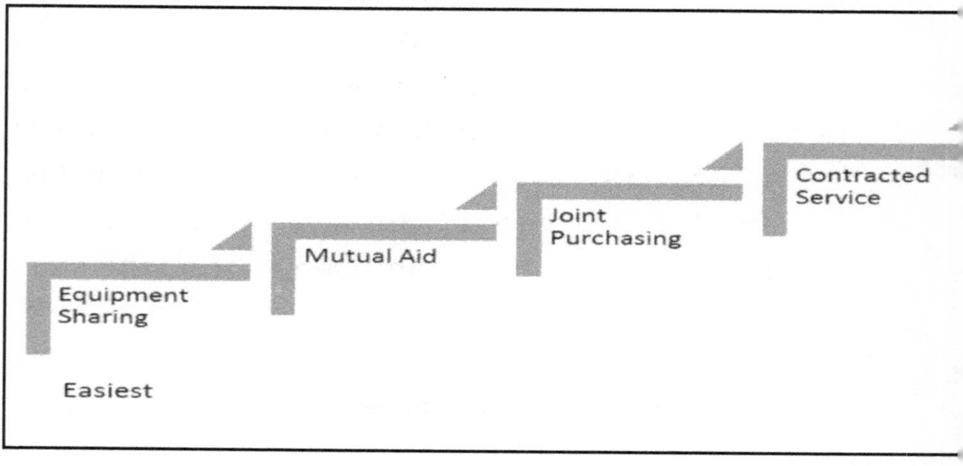

Contracted Service

Joint Purchasing

Mutual Aid

Equipment Sharing

Easiest

and maintain a high level of services in the face of ever-shrinking revenues. Shared service arrangements come in many forms and are a time-tested alternative to municipal service delivery that has proven to be cost effective. One county in Wisconsin has created over 100 shared service efforts, both internally and externally, in an attempt to contain costs.

Shared service options range from relatively simple handshake arrangements to complex, intergovernmental agreements, to the full consolidation of governmental units. These options are depicted in Fig. 1.

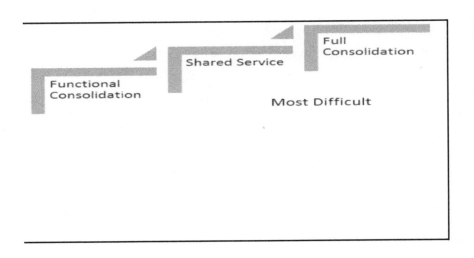

As one climbs up the hill of shared service opportunities, the process becomes more and more difficult and complex.

Each of the elements in Figure 1 is discussed briefly below.

EQUIPMENT SHARING

For years, public works departments have been ahead of the curve when it comes to equipment sharing. For example, they would often provide a brush chipper, spare plow, backhoe, street sweeper, etc. to a neighboring municipality with nothing more than a handshake between two public works superintendents. A shared service arrangement that avoids bureaucratic complexity.

An early and more complex form of equipment sharing between municipalities occurred in the early 1980s as the computer age was on the horizon. At that time, there was little or no software for municipal payroll or other financial operations. The most affordable computers were "mini-computers," which were the size of small refrigerators and had "dumb" terminals (i.e., with all data on disks or platters in the minicomputer). If the disks got a glitch, the computer system—and the work—came to a halt.

In an effort to automate office procedures to do more (and do it better, faster and cheaper), a group of eight municipalities (originally 10, but two dropped out of the process) in southeast Wisconsin got together to discuss more efficient alternatives. These were small municipalities ranging in population from 1,600 to 18,000—none of which could afford the cost of automating administrative services on their own.

It was determined that by working together, hardware could be purchased (joint purchasing) and software could be obtained (joint software development). If the new machines didn't work right, they had each other to rely on for support since all had identical hardware and software. Thus, an organization called Southeast Urban Data Systems (SUDS) was born. Not only were the computers less expensive to obtain through bulk purchasing, but the software was designed to be identical in each municipality.

The software shared within SUDS included programs for general ledger, payroll, accounts payable, tax billing, voter registration, utility billing and word processing. These eight municipalities entered the computer age! If a system crashed, municipality A could turn to municipality B for assistance with those functions where time was of the essence. It was an early form of the backup system. Sure enough, shortly after implementation one of the municipality's computer systems crashed on a Thursday, with payroll checks due the next day (there was no automatic deposit in those days). Try not paying your employees once and see what happens. Things get ugly in a hurry!

The payroll data that was stored on a backup floppy disk, was taken to the neighboring participating municipality along with a supply of blank checks. Friday arrived, and everyone got paid. The concept worked!

All of this was done through a combination of shared service concepts:

- Common program development (software)
- Joint purchasing (hardware)
- Functional consolidation (internal services)
- Mutual aid (backup system)
- Intergovernmental agreements

The above effort saved each of the eight municipalities thousands of dollars, allowed them to do more work (better, faster and cheaper) and brought them into the computer age in a very cost-effective manner.

MUTUAL AID

Mutual aid agreements are plans for the sharing of resources between communities during an emergency or disaster. They address legal, technical, and procedural issues such as:

- When and how to request assistance
- Reimbursement procedures

- License requirements
- Certification and permit portability
- Workers' compensation coverage, insurance, and liability

Mutual aid occurs automatically when an emergency arises. Fire departments have taken the lead in developing the mutual aid concept, and other emergency services have followed suit.

Mutual aid functions are found among almost all municipal organizations, with police and fire departments being the most common. Typically, mutual aid groups are free to join and participate in, and all activities are voluntary. They are often structured as non-hierarchical, non-bureaucratic and non-profit organizations, with members controlling all resources and with no external financial or professional support. They are member-led and member-organized. They are egalitarian in nature and designed to support participatory democracy, equality of member status, power-shared leadership and cooperative decision-making. Members' external societal status is considered irrelevant inside the group; status in the group is conferred by participation.

JOINT PURCHASING
Municipalities have been participating in joint purchasing programs for many years. The faltering

national economy in 2008 put added pressure on everyone's budget—from families to major corporations. State and local governments were feeling the pinch as well. Those who did the purchasing for government agencies had always looked for the best ways to get the lowest possible prices for the many goods and services municipalities must procure. At that time, there was even more pressure to squeeze every tax dollar to obtain the best value possible.

Needless to say, municipal professionals have always strived to scrutinize every purchase, use best practice standards, and watch how pennies are spent. The search for lower costs, greater efficiency, and improved product quality never ends. It is what has always been demanded of them, but especially when the country is in the midst of a recession that reaches all levels of government.

There are a number of ways that state and local governments have worked together to realize significant savings in purchasing. These programs and initiatives were in development prior to the country's recent economic woes, but they are timelier today than ever before. State and local agencies in a cooperative program have tremendous combined buying power. By bidding a contract as a cooperative agreement, the state gains leverage through volume-driven cost reductions.

1. SHARED SERVICES DEFINED

Before entering into any cooperative contract, the purchasing agency evaluates the proposed contract very thoroughly, along with the prospects for savings. They consider the impact such a contract would have on the local business environment as compared to what can be gained from using a Total Cost of Ownership model (utilizing the benefits of a broad-based standard set of specifications). Total Cost of Ownership takes into consideration not only the original purchase price but ongoing operating costs and estimated residual value at the end of useful life.

The sheer number of states involved in such initiatives means that vendors realize they must be very aggressive in pricing in order to win bids and gain large volume contracts. Purchasing cooperatives can identify which of the services and/or commodities might best fit participants' needs in order to take advantage of leverage opportunities.

Municipalities joining with their state purchasing cooperatives and bidding like items has proven to result in both the overall lowest unit price and the lowest total cost of ownership across the entire supply chain (considering the cost of freight and soft costs). Participation in such regional cooperatives will open up more contract opportunities for local governments.

Additionally, as permitted by statute, states are now negotiating more of their vendor contracts.

States are also taking a more aggressive approach to negotiating contract extensions. These contracts are then made available to local units of government.

Joint purchasing has become a common form of shared services that has generated little if any controversy, but it has proven to offer better value at a lower cost to taxpayers.

CONTRACTED SERVICES (OUTSOURCING)

Contracted services occur when one entity obtains a service for a fee from another entity through a formal written agreement in which one independent party provides a defined service to an independent recipient party. Most municipalities enter into numerous contracts for services each year, ranging from relatively simple services to complex undertakings. This usually occurs when the service provider is more experienced at providing a specific function.

FUNCTIONAL CONSOLIDATION

Functional consolidation is the combining of separate functions or services into a single one, usually where one organization is more efficient or better suited to providing a function. This often occurs among a municipality's "backroom functions" such as payroll, purchasing, external hiring, etc.

SHARED SERVICES (JOINT VENTURE)

As previously mentioned, a shared service is the provision of a service by one part of an organization or group where that service had previously been found in more than one part of the organization or group. Thus, the funding and resourcing of the service is shared—and the providing department effectively becomes an internal service provider.

The key here is the idea of "sharing" within an organization or group. This sharing needs to fundamentally include shared accountability of results by the unit from which the work was migrated to the provider. The provider, on the other hand, needs to ensure that results are delivered based on defined, agreed-upon measures. This joint venture involves the creation of a separate legal commercial entity (jointly owned), which provides necessary oversight of the effort.

FULL CONSOLIDATION

Full consolidation is the legal joining together of two or more separate entities into a newly formed single entity in order to provide a specific service or range of services. The separate organizations no longer exist and are replaced by a single entity.

All of these efforts to save tax dollars should be on the radar screen of governmental professionals as they consider how best to maximize the use of those funds.

CHAPTER 2

CHALLENGES AND OPPORTUNITIES

"Coming together is a beginning; keeping together is progress; working together is success."
—Henry Ford

Almost all elected officials serve their communities on a part-time basis and do not have expertise in the inner workings of the organization over which they are expected to promote effective public policy and/or make informed policy decisions. When it comes to the complex topic of shared services, the natural tendency of most elected officials is to turn to the professionals on their staffs for information, advice and recommendations. These are often the only available sources of information unless an independent third-party analysis has already been conducted.

Since most municipalities are change-adverse (and most department directors are even more so), the first response from most municipal directors is to recommend against most shared service opportunities. The result is that many shared service efforts die before getting meaningful consideration. Why is this so? There are a variety of reasons, including loss of control, loss of personnel, loss of identity, loss of individual stature, and the fear of the unknown (change).

LOSS OF CONTROL

A department director is hired to operate a department to the best of his/her ability. To do so, most directors feel that they need direct control over the employees as well as the policies and procedures of their departments. The natural tendency of most directors is to resist sharing this authority with another entity, board, or commission. They feel that their authority and responsibilities will be diluted by combining their operation with another organization.

A director may also believe that such a change will result in a loss of stature in the organization, among colleagues and in the community. "This is not the way we do things" is a common attitude when the subject of shared services is broached. In many instances, this has a great deal to do with personal ego.

Equally challenging, elected officials may view a shared service effort as placing the service (and subsequent service level provided) outside of their control, thus making it more difficult to influence and impact the services being provided, control expenses or control the individual managing the service. This feels unnatural to many elected officials who feel a responsibility to maintain control over municipal services. After all, that's what he/she was elected to do.

Recently, two small municipalities were in need of a new street sweeper but did not feel they could afford to purchase one due to its cost for the limited number of streets the municipalities were responsible for sweeping. One of the municipalities suggested that they jointly purchase a street sweeper for them both to use. The neighboring community considered the offer, and the city council referred the idea to their public works committee for consideration and to work out the details. The two municipalities agreed to share the acquisition and maintenance costs equally; however, the discussions got bogged down over who would be the equipment operator, how much the operator would be paid, and who would get to use it first.

The two public works directors could not agree on who would be the sweeper operator, with each fearing they would lose control if they did not have their own operator doing the street sweeping. If there was to be only one operator from each municipality and the sweeper was damaged or not properly maintained, each director feared a loss of control over discipline and routine maintenance issues.

The elected officials on each respective public works committee expressed concern about who would have first use of the sweeper after the important post-winter street cleaning operations. Neither wanted to wait until mid-summer to have the sweeper available. This loss of control could result in poor street sweeping service and would not sit well with their respective constituents.

The deal fell apart over the issue of loss of control.

LOSS OF PERSONNEL

In many instances, a shared service opportunity will result in staff reductions for one or more entities involved in the effort. This is common and to be expected. Invariably, entities have excess labor capacity to take on additional tasks, as seldom are the employees in any given department always working at full capacity 100 percent of the time. As a result, some of the workload in a shared service effort can be absorbed by existing staff. While some employees of the precious stand-alone effort may be absorbed in the new entity, as is frequently the case, some employees may lose their jobs.

There are two consequences to staff reductions. First, this may be viewed by the department director as a reduction in his "empire." If the director has fewer staff to supervise, it may create the potential for smaller salary increases for the director because the department for which he is responsible is now smaller.

Second, staff reductions may mean employee layoffs. Unlike the private sector, the public sector tends to be very averse to laying off employees. For whatever reason, municipalities have developed a "secure employment" philosophy. In the current era of limited resources, municipal officials should take a more businesslike approach to staff.

Recently, a city manager determined that the city's internal, one-person print shop was operating inefficiently. The print shop employee was supervised by the city clerk, who did not view the city's printing needs as a priority and thus paid little attention to the print ship operations. The equipment was old, out of date, and needed replacement.

Departments, on the other hand, were frustrated with response times. If printing orders were received from several departments at the same time, and, with only one print shop employee, there were frequent delays in order processing.

After surveying the printing needs of all of the departments in the city, it was discovered that much of the print work was already being outsourced. When the city manager analyzed the salary, benefits, and cost of equipment replacement, it was determined that the most cost-effective alternative was to outsource all of the city's printing needs. To do so meant that the long-time print shop employee would need to be laid off.

The city manager presented a plan to the city council to entirely eliminate in-house printing. To do so, the city would sell or scrap the existing equipment and turn the print shop area into a much-needed storage area for old files. He also reported that the print shop employee would be laid off. The result would be a net cost savings of approximately $85,000 per year, which would be the difference between the elimination of the wages and benefits of the one print shop employee and the cost of outsourced printing.

The city council liked the idea of saving money and applauded the city manager for his imaginative effort in this instance. However, they did not like the idea of laying off employees, which they had never done before. Council members struggled with the foreign concept of losing personnel through layoffs. Sensing that his entire plan might be lost over the layoff issue, the city manager suggested—and the council finally agreed—that there be a delay in the closing of the print shop and that the city manager would negotiate an early retirement for the print shop employee.

This was done, and the print shop was closed, but the loss of personnel through layoffs nearly derailed the city manager's effort to save tax dollars because the city council had a "secure employment" philosophy.

LOSS OF IDENTITY

A place (i.e., a city, village, or town) is a location of social pride. People identify with their community as their home in order to identify where they live and, to some degree, to describe their living style. At the 4th of July parade, they like seeing fire trucks and police cars with the community's name emblazoned on the side of the vehicle. This invokes a sense of community pride, which is a good thing.

But when it comes to discussions of shared services, this sense of community pride can become a roadblock to a specific group or groups within the community—primarily the elected and appointed officials.

In an emergency, when residents need services immediately, they become less concerned about the name on the side of the vehicles providing them services. They only desire a needed service, and they want it now! This is not the sentiment of elected officials, and it's even less that of department directors. These community groups want everyone to know it is their community providing residents these services and that it's their tax dollars at work. That is why a great deal of effort and tax dollars are spent putting bold designs on the sides of municipal vehicles, announcing exactly who is being served by whom. Eliminating names and logos on municipal vehicles might not be the answer, but as unmarked police cars have already demonstrated, the officer inside can get the job done as well as another officer in a marked car (if not better).

Once a fire chief was questioned about the cost of gold-leaf lettering and striping on the side of his fire trucks. His explanation of the value of this cost to the community was, "It looks really cool and makes our department stand out in parades." When asked if it helps his station fight fires, he said, "No. But it helps to create pride within our department."

While creating pride in the community and in the departments that provide the services within the community is valuable, it should not get in the way of operating better, faster, or cheaper—which is often the end result. Frequently elected officials and department directors fail to focus on their core functions out of a fear that they will lose identity (and, in the process, quite possibly their own identity).

CHANGE AND FEAR OF THE UNKNOWN

Municipalities, by nature, are change averse. There is a general fear of the unknown and a comfort in maintaining the status quo. Unlike in the private sector, where new ideas are introduced in the boardroom behind closed doors, public change is developed, discussed, negotiated, and made in a fishbowl for all to see. In fact, it is more than a fishbowl; it's a large aquarium with sharks lurking in the shadows, waiting to take advantage of a potential mistake. Elected officials worry about those sharks (their opponents and the electorate). They worry, "What will residents think of me if this change does not work? Will I get reelected? Will services diminish? Will people feel left out? Do I have to lay off employees? "These are all fears of the unknown.

The path to shared services is difficult, time consuming and full of opposition. Elected officials as part-time policymakers may not have the time and energy to invest in such a process and bring it to a successful conclusion—so the easier path is often to continue to do things as they have always been done.

> Gordon Parks, the 1970s civil rights documentary filmmaker, once said, "The guy who takes a chance, who walks the line between the known and the unknown, who is unafraid of failure, will succeed."

This is also a safer bet for those fearing they will be called out and held responsible if a new program doesn't work.

For difficult issues, a frequent approach by elected officials is to put the question of shared services to a referendum and let the citizens decide what they want and how they want their services provided. This is not only a move to pass the buck by officials who were elected to make the difficult decisions, but because these issues are complex, it is unrealistic to expect citizens to take the time and effort to understand all of the nuances of shared services and make an informed decision. Therefore, the result is often a continuation of the status quo. Public officials should be willing to make the difficult decisions.

This is what they were elected to do!

CHAPTER 3
SUCCESSES AND FAILURES

"The price of success is hard work, dedication to the job at hand, and the determination that whether we win or lose, we have applied the best of ourselves to the task at hand."
—Vince Lombardi,
Green Bay Packers Football Coach

I f developing and implementing shared service arrangements in the municipal setting was easy, everyone would be doing it. More municipalities would be operating more efficiently, and large amounts of tax dollars would be saved (and there would be no need for this book). As already noted, it is an arduous, politically challenging and time-consuming process. The process is full of political pitfalls, which many politicians who are weak of heart may try to avoid. Some have tried, some have succeeded, and many have failed.

As an example, in 2013, a fire service consolidation in five municipalities (and dispatch consolidation in three of these municipalities) was considered. The municipalities followed the typical approach of retaining the services of an independent body (in this case, a regional independent think tank) to weigh the pros and cons of consolidation. All factors in the existing approach to providing services were compared to how they might provide services within a shared service model. The think tank organization analyzed staffing, equipment, operating costs, capital costs, station location, response times, management structure and organizational structure. In the case of the analysis of fire consolidation, it was estimated that the municipalities could save more than $800,000 in operating costs and $1.7 million in capital costs—a significant amount of money in any budget.

The municipalities did not consolidate their fire departments or dispatch centers. While they already shared expertise and provided mutual aid to each other, the issues of leadership (*Who will be the chief?*), governance (*Will my community lose control?*), personnel (*Will people lose their jobs?*) and change (*What if it fails?*) trumped the opportunity to save tax dollars. This is a typical result.

In 1995, at the opposite end of the same county, seven municipalities, after lengthy analysis and consideration, successfully combined their fire departments into a single department. What was the difference?

While substantial savings were present in both instances, there were significant practical circumstances that made the difference. In the case of the

1995 effort, each community had a professional municipal manager. They all met regularly on a variety of municipal issues over a long period of time, which resulted in a very collegial atmosphere among them. They trusted each other. In addition, the chief elected officials (mayors and village presidents) who also met regularly, creating an atmosphere of trust among them as well.

Even more importantly, these elected officials demonstrated strong political leadership among each other, their elected bodies, and their respective citizens. When they found a better way of doing things to benefit the community and their taxpayers, they made it happen even in the face of strong opposition from citizens and unions. Furthermore, there was a history of working together on a variety of municipal challenges. Some of the communities shared a municipal water supply, others shared emergency dispatch services, and still others shared recreation programs. They recognized the benefits of these opportunities in which to work together.

As these seven communities began to study the concept of merging their fire departments, they took several unique courses of action to achieve their goal. First, they created a study committee that consisted of the chief-elected official from each municipality. However, rather than haggle over who would chair this committee, they engaged the services of a local respected citizen, who was also an attorney, to serve as an independent committee chair. This individual had no political agenda and was able to keep the discussions focused and on track without offending any of the stakeholders.

Second, not only were all of the meetings published as public meetings, but specific invitations were sent to the fire department unions to attend the study committee meetings and be active participants. It was recognized early on that it would be important to have the support of the current firefighters in order to be successful. Therefore, their input throughout the process was important. The firefighter representatives raised many concerns throughout the process, and these concerns were addressed to the extent possible without sacrificing important management and policy positions. At the very least, the firefighters felt their concerns were addressed and that they were being heard.

Third, two of the communities had previously experienced major fires in commercial buildings. In post-fire analyses, it was demonstrated that the fires were not handled particularly well and that the mutual aid system that was in place lacked a strong leadership structure and firefighting plan to effectively respond to large structure fires.

These factors, along with a projected substantial cost savings, resulted in the creation of one fire department that previously consisted of full-time departments, volunteer departments, and one public safety department. Combining diverse organizational structures is one of the most challenging aspects of a shared service effort. However, once again this challenge was overcome through the recognition that there was a better, faster and cheaper way to provide fire and EMS services to these communities.

There are six keys to a successful consolidation approach, which build upon each other and are all necessary to obtain positive results. Any break in the six keys severely weakens the potential that the shared service effort will succeed. These keys are outlined in Fig. 2 below.

VISION AND TRUST
Strong political leadership by top elected officials in each participating municipality in a shared service initiative is a must. These political leaders must also have a vision for doing things better and recognize

Figure 2: Necessary keys for the development and implementation of a successful shared service program

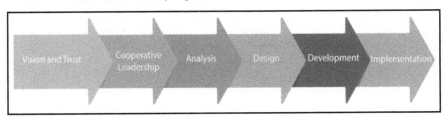

that current methodologies are not sustainable over the long run. Along with a vision for working better, faster and cheaper, they also need to be working with colleagues that they trust. They must trust that their colleagues will do the right things and put personal and/or parochial community benefits aside for the greater good.

Shared services, by their very nature, require a cultural change and a divergence from business as usual. When attempting to introduce cultural change and new ways of working, it is important to get mindsets right at all levels of the organization in order to win people over. In addition to setting up the "nuts and bolts" of project and performance management processes, the project manager, working alongside senior officers, needs to invest time in setting out the rules of engagement. They should also ensure there is understanding and agreement that the project is about the greater good of the region rather than silos working and competing with neighboring authorities.

COOPERATIVE LEADERSHIP

Strong political leadership is important for a successful shared service program. Leaders should know each other and have a comfort level in working with each other, and it is helpful when there are previous examples of successful cooperative efforts. Regular meetings of chief-elected officials lead to a heightened sense of camaraderie and cooperation.

Many chief-elected officials are part time and do not bring personal agendas to the position. They run for office to make a difference in their communities and provide guidance and leadership to their elected boards. This is important during any shared service initiative, as many decisions require a leap of faith to cooperate with other communities.

Strong leadership is essential for the credibility, organizational focus and staff motivation of regional shared service opportunities. There are four main qualities that distinguish effective collaborative leaders:

1. They combine tremendous persistence, energy and resolve with a measured (limited) ego.

2. They are passionate about the desired outcome and will work diligently to achieve their goals.

3. They pull others along rather than push them in the desired direction.

4. They think systematically and are focused on the greater good.

To achieve success, good collaborative leaders must also:

- Create excitement about the purpose of the shared service effort being undertaken.

- Be effective at getting the right people around the table and keeping them involved and committed.

- Help players find the common interests and mutual benefits possible only through joint efforts.

- Generate trust between and among the players (this is important above all else).

- Help design a transparent, credible process that is inclusive of all stakeholders involved.

- Focus on the win-win. All parties must be winners.

- Make relationship-building a priority for the group.

- Ensure senior champions are at the table and directly involved.

- Engage everyone in collaborative problem-solving discussions.

- Celebrate small successes and share credit widely.

- Provide confidence, hope, guidance and resilience.

ANALYSIS

Conducting an in-depth objective analysis is not sexy and is often boring, but it is a necessary component of a fruitful shared-service effort. Public decisions must be data driven, and the information being used to make decisions must be objective. This portion of a shared service project almost always requires the assistance of outside professionals that do not represent any single entity and are skilled in data collection and analysis. These consultants provide objective analyses that decision makers feel comfortable relying on.

Too often, internal analyses are conducted by department heads. They show how efficient their departments already are, thereby dissuading elected officials from shared services that may impact their departments in a manner they view as undesirable. While it is not difficult to slant or selectively use data to support a position, it may not be objective. This is the core of the turf battles that occur in almost every shared service effort.

DESIGN

Organizational design provides the ongoing structure that leads to the ultimate success of the newly designed organization, and it is the most important component of a shared service effort. If it is designed poorly at the outset, it will perform poorly and will lead to its ultimate and likely early demise.

Creating an effective design structure often requires outside assistance from professionals skilled in organizational development. There are a variety of factors that must be considered in the design component, including management structure, staffing levels, scheduling, pay and benefits, reporting relationships and intergovernmental agreements. Failure to properly address any of these necessary components will create weak links that opponents will take advantage of in order to cause the shared service to fail.

The design stage of a shared service requires intense attention to detail in order to prevent mistakes and failure in service delivery. To assist in the avoidance of these pitfalls, a list of questions has been developed to assist in making sure that the effort is successful. The list that follows (Figure 3) is not intended to be all-inclusive. Instead, it is a guide to build upon for each organization's individual needs—and a start for those who do not know where or how to begin the process.

Figure 3: Service Design Questions

Identity	Operating Model	Organization	People	Processes
What is the history of the shared services in the organization?	What is the current operating and service delivery model?	How will it be structured, and who will lead what parts?	What is the culture of the organization? What are its key values and behaviors?	What are the shared services processes?
When is it to be established and implemented	Which parts of the service will be shared, and which will be kept within the organization?	How are the teams to be organized? What are their functions?	What are the key workforce competencies? Do we have them?	What will help customers understand the processes and engage with the organization?
Where is it to be located?	Where will managers and staff be physically located?	How will the organization be managed?	How will staff be recruited/ retained?	What reports will be produced, and what is their purpose, content, timing, etc.
What is the organization's vision for the future?	What are the customer contact channels, and how are queries resolved?	How are the organization's relationships with its partners determined?	How will staff be trained and developed?	What are the standards for data and document management, including retention and destruction?
What is the shared service's core purpose?	What will be included in the intergovernmental agreement?	What are the agreed service levels and success metrics? Have benchmarks been set?	Do we have the expertise to develop measurable metrics?	How will information be stored and accessed?
What are the organization's primary objectives?	Will there be third-party involvement? To what extent	What service charges and penalties will there be?	Who will be responsible for monitoring activities?	Will security standards be necessary?
What are the key principles by which the program will operate?	Is there an existing system that can be used as a model?	Is there a business continuity plan in place?	Does the organization have skilled contract managers?	Are there audit checks and reporting systems for management in place?

DEVELOPMENT

Once the new organization is activated, the "design" becomes an ongoing process of continuous improvement and modification to adjust for unforeseen circumstances. As the organization matures, new opportunities will present themselves for further improvements. Leadership and management need to be watchful for these opportunities. This often requires additional management and staff training.

A long-range and flexible strategic plan needs to be created and followed. Again, strategic plans need the support of top elected officials and/or the responsible oversight board in order to be workable and followed. Otherwise, strategic plans may become a required exercise that results in no more than a plan collecting dust on a shelf.

IMPLEMENTATION

Once all the required pieces are in place, it becomes time to "flip the switch" and make the shared service initiative operational. Prior to this happening, the new management team should develop a checklist of operational needs to make sure that all contingencies are considered. This requires, at a minimum, that:

- Proper staffing and scheduling are in place
- The staff is fully trained
- Equipment is in place and operational

- Policies and procedures have been developed and are in place
- Technical systems are operational (hardware, software, records systems, etc.)
- The entire management team is available to immediately address unforeseen challenges

During the first week of operations, a status report should be made to the oversight board, indicating how well events did or did not go, unexpected challenges that occurred and an overall assessment of the operation. This will help create a sense of confidence in management and in the success of the new endeavor. It will also create a foundation of trust between management and the oversight body that can be further developed as time goes on.

CHAPTER 4
PERSONNEL ISSUES

"Thunder is impressive, but it is lightning that does the work."
—Mark Twain

A t the heart of every department and organization are the employees who provide the services, respond to citizens, and make the system work. When an organization is considering a shared service opportunity, those same employees will, in all likelihood, respond very negatively. After all, a majority of department costs are typically personnel costs—and if the goal is to reduce costs, that typically means there will be fewer positions in the new entity (or at the very least, a major department restructuring).

If the organization is unionized, the unions will immediately begin a campaign in opposition to any changes. Bear in mind that the number-one purpose of a union is to protect the jobs of its members. If the head of the impacted department is not on board, he/she will oppose the shared service as well (as explained in the next chapter on turf protection) and may even be supportive of union efforts.

So what are typical employee concerns and how can they be addressed? They usually include the following:

- Will I lose my job?
- Will my work location change, and will I have to drive farther to get to work?
- Will my pay be affected? If so, how?
- Will my benefits change?
- What will happen to my vacation and sick time benefits and time-off accumulations?
- Will retirement benefits change?
- Will my work schedule change?
- How will my seniority be affected?
- Will I be represented by a union? If multiple unions are involved, which one?
- Who will I be working with, and will I be able to work well with them?
- Who will my supervisor be, and will I be able to work with him/her?
- Will opportunities for promotion be greater or less as a result of a department merger?
- Will I have to invest time to be retrained?
- What will be the policies and procedures of the new organization?
- This is change, and I don't like change.
- I am afraid of the unknown.

The list goes on and on, but do not be mistaken—these are all very real and serious issues to employees. Their concerns need to be addressed very early on in the discussion phase and on an ongoing basis throughout the process.

People issues are compounded if the entities under consideration are not only unionized, but also represented by several different unions with different contract provisions. Addressing this challenge will be discussed in detail later in this chapter.

As the process of a shared service is initiated, management should meet with their respective employees before information becomes public. It is wise to explain to employees that while they have been doing an excellent job in providing services (assuming this is in fact the case), business as usual is not sustainable and alternative service delivery options are being investigated due to a number of financial, managerial, and political reasons. No preconceived conclusions have been determined, and no decisions have been made. The process is in the investigative stage only, and regular updates will be provided to employees as the process progresses.

While this sounds good at the outset, it is only the beginning of this very important communication and trust-building process. It is essential that management take additional steps.

First, it is likely that the meetings between the shared service departments will be public meetings—but even if they are not, rank-and-file employees should be invited to attend. This is especially beneficial if the departments are unionized. It will not be enough to simply say at the outset that the union is welcome to attend. They should be sent a notice, agenda, and study information for each and every meeting.

The union and/or employees need not necessarily be made a part of the study committee, although this might be beneficial in some circumstances. In any event, they should be given the opportunity to speak and raise their concerns at each meeting. The study committee is not obligated to respond to or resolve each issue as it is raised, but employees need to feel that they are being heard and that their concerns will be addressed.

Also, the study committee needs to be cognizant of the fact that while the views of employees and the union are important, they cannot be allowed to dominate the discussion. Managing this may require strong leadership by the committee chair. Depending on the makeup of the committee or employee groups present, one approach is to provide time at some point during the meeting (with specific time limitations) for employee groups to present their concerns.

Also, if a union is involved, a three-party dynamic might be created, which can complicate discussions. The study committee is typically made up of management, and the union may have two interests—that of the union members (employees) and of the union itself (union leadership). The study committee needs to be aware of this as discussions proceed and be sure that in the end it is the employees' interests that are at the forefront of decisions.

The bottom line is that during the study phase of any shared service, management cannot communicate enough. When they think they have addressed employee concerns, they should check with those employees to be sure. Providing too much information is better than providing too little in most cases.

UNION CONTRACT ISSUES

Let's assume for a moment that management has made the decision to enter into a shared service arrangement. As an illustration, four municipalities have decided to join their public works departments to create a single, consolidated entity. The consolidated department will have a single public works director, who will report to a management committee made up of one representative from each of the four municipalities. In this example, the original four separate departments were unionized, but each was represented by a different union. Therefore, each of the old departments had a union contract, and these differed widely from each other. They had different job titles and duties, different pay and benefit structures, different promotion processes, and different management rights. One union may have had higher pay rates but fewer benefits. Another may have had a more generous health insurance program. A third union may have had stronger impacts on management rights.

These issues need to be addressed and resolved very carefully, because decisions made at the beginning of a new venture will impact the organization for many years to come. In this instance, the first step in the unionization process would be for the consolidated organization to determine which union will represent employees (i.e., the employees must decide through a union election process which union will represent them). While this is not a responsibility of management, it is a step that must be completed by the employees before any discussions of wages, benefits, or conditions of employment can begin.

While this process of union organization is being conducted, management must spend time reviewing existing contract provisions and comparing and contrasting the differences among the existing contracts. This is necessary because as the new union submits its initial proposal for a new union contract, it will invariably select the provisions most advantageous to the union and those most generous to employees. This is a process called "cherry-picking."

Management needs to be cognizant of "cherry-picking" from the outset and not react negatively, because it is just a part of the process. Unions understand that if they don't ask for a benefit or a management right, it won't be offered voluntarily and they won't get it. They also understand that they will not get everything they ask for, but there is no harm in asking.

During the union contract negotiation process, previous contracts typically serve as the basis for negotiating new provisions. In the case of a newly created organization where there is no previous contract, the process begins with a clean slate—and every provision of the new contract must be negotiated and agreed upon. This is not to say that a number of provisions from previous contracts won't be used; however, there is no requirement or expectation that any previous contract language will be included in the new contract. Negotiating an initial contract is extremely important, because it will become the foundation for all future contracts. This is one of the few times that union contract negotiations begin from square one.

The most difficult provisions to negotiate will always be job positions, wages, and benefits, because they will seldom match among the previous contracts of the separate entities. For example, the separate departments may have previously had positions of laborer, street worker, and facility maintenance—all of which was essentially the same work. Union and management must initially agree on job titles by either selecting one of the existing titles or creating new ones and putting that class of employees collectively into that category.

In other instances, one of the departments may have had a job title that none of the other departments had. Union and management must either agree to continue that job title or reclassify those employees into one of the agreed-upon titles.

Once job titles are determined, the process of determining wages and benefits will begin. The union will seek the highest pay rate found among the separate contracts. Should management seek to negotiate the lowest pay rate? Caution must be exercised here. Attempting to get the union to agree to the lowest pay rate can result in the loss of employees who quickly become disgruntled with the new organization. Worse yet, employee morale could dip so low that employees will work to undermine the success of the newly consolidated department.

A better approach is for management to conduct a wage-and-benefit survey and negotiate pay and benefit rates that are at or near market value.

Once wages are agreed upon, there may be some employees who get a pay reduction under the new pay plan. Is it reasonable to reduce employee pay? Probably not, in most cases. Nothing makes an employee more disgruntled than to be paid less in a new organization than he/she was getting previously. A common solution to this issue is to "red-circle" those employees. This means that they will not have their pay reduced; instead, it will be frozen at its current rate until such time as the pay scale for employees in the same pay category catches up with or exceeds the employee's frozen rate of pay. While those employees may not be entirely satisfied, it is much less painful and less disruptive to the overall organization than cutting someone's rate of pay.

Health insurance is an equally difficult issue to resolve. Employees are averse to changing doctors and health-insurance carriers with changing benefits. If management is not cognizant of the myriad benefits available in the marketplace and their impact on employees and costs, it may be money well spent to hire an outside professional to assist in resolving health-benefit and health-insurance provider issues.

Caution must be exercised for all the other provisions of the initial union contract such as management rights, promotion procedures, training requirements, overtime assignments, etc. Undoubtedly, the consolidated department will have a whole new set of employee policies and procedures. Remember that what is negotiated in the initial union contract will become the foundation for all future contracts. Management should take its time and thoughtfully consider each contract provision carefully. There should be no need to rush through this process.

Union contract negotiations will likely begin before the consolidated department begins to operate—but because it often takes an exceedingly long time to negotiate this initial contract, it may not be approved in time to coincide with the implementation of the consolidated department. In this case, the initiation of operations should not be delayed. Employees should work with the wages, benefits, and conditions of employment they received from their predecessor organization until a new union contract is ratified. This may put pressure on management to try to ratify a union contract as soon as possible, but careful and prudent negotiations should outweigh the desire to obtain a new union contract too quickly.

CHAPTER 5
MY TURF OR YOUR TURF?

"Nearly all men can stand adversity,
but if you want to test a man's character,
give him power."
—Abraham Lincoln

In almost every instance of attempted shared service efforts, there is a perceived loss of control by both department heads and elected officials when two or more municipalities are involved. There is an inclination to protect one's turf before the facts can be developed and analyzed.

The typical department director's response to the city manager or city council is concern that if he/she cannot tell the building inspector what to do (i.e., leadership and direction) in a consolidated inspections department, he/she will be uncertain that work is getting done (analysis of outcomes).

Addressing this concern is twofold. First, there must be recognition that the outcomes of a consolidated organization are the same or better than those of separate municipal departments. Second, consolidation may mean utilizing new and different processes and working through a new entity (a new committee or commission) which may serve as the director's new "boss."

Managers in the public sector feel very comfortable in the process mode, as opposed to the policy mode. This is because the politicians at the local level make the strategy decisions, and the managers competently establish the processes to implement them.

The first step managers frequently take in designing shared services is to begin an examination and benchmarking of each partner's current service processes compared to their own. If each partner's service has some elements of best practices, then a good partnership will likely result. Everyone wins by bringing together the "good" from each to build a collaborative best practice.

However, this search for best practices does not take into account the attitudes, feelings, and culture of the organization, directors and personnel involved in the shared service/consolidation effort. This is usually the source of all turf wars and should be addressed early on in any effort.

There is typically a great fear of the unknown by existing department employees. They may ask themselves such questions as:

- Will my department be reduced in size?
- Will I have to lay off employees?

- Will my salary be reduced/frozen?
- Will I have less influence with policymakers?
- Will my reputation as a department leader be negatively impacted?
- If this does not work, will I get blamed?
- What will others think of me?

In the rush to proceed with the tasks at hand, the personnel impacts of turf can easily be neglected—or ignored completely. Typically, the needs of any group that touches or is touched by the service under review should be considered. These are the customers of the service (internal to your organization, as well as external customers), such as:

- The staff who work within the service
- The managers of the service under consideration
- Elected officials and board/commission members
- Impacted unions
- Other potential third parties and community organizations

Typically, at the first hint of an organization considering any shared service effort, department directors and employees immediately begin circling the wagons and developing arguments about why the effort will not work. The arguments will be laced with facts, statistics, costs, and anecdotal examples (sometimes with enriched circumstances to support the cause against the consolidation).

In order to "win" the turf war, a number of steps need to be taken—and a couple things must be avoided. First, a study team must be created that has strong political leadership from the elected body, as well as management support from the chief administrative officer. The director (department head) of the department(s) most directly impacted should be on the study committee as well, as they are the closest to the issues and challenges at hand.

The meetings of this study team should be open to the public. Additionally, a conscious and overt effort should be made to invite the impacted department employees and/or union representatives to attend. The latter need not be included on the study committee, but opportunities for their input should be made available at each meeting.

The process must be controlled by management. The impacted departments will almost always approach the issue negatively for a variety of reasons, including the fear of the unknown, loss of jobs, and reduced authority (turf). The study team must be prepared to respond to negative comments, operational attacks, and emotional discourse. Employees and members of the public may well pose vitriolic charges against any shared service effort. Comments such as the following have been heard during some shared-service study committee meetings:

- If we consolidate our emergency dispatch services, the new dispatchers will not know the district. This will result in delays, and babies will die!
- If the fire departments are consolidated, the firefighters will quit!
- If the inspection departments are consolidated, inspections will be delayed and cause builders to go elsewhere!
- If we consolidate, the department director will have a lack of control and oversight.

The arguments go on and on. The employees (and at times, department directors) will often ignore the normal responses and everyday workloads and dig through past records to present one or two anecdotal incidents that support their position as evidence that the shared service under consideration will never work.

In one actual study of an emergency dispatch consolidation effort, the police chief, who was vehemently opposed to a consolidation effort, reported that one of his local dispatchers recognized the voice of a caller who had previously been involved in another incident and was able to name the individual, reducing the time for a police apprehension. While this may have actually happened, the flaw in the argument is twofold. First, the dispatchers in a large unit would have more dispatchers who could recognize the voices of more callers. Second, this incident occurred prior to emergency-call-triangulation technology, which now accurately pinpoints call locations and often caller ID.

Part of the turf issue often focuses on where the service will be provided (i.e., *My place or yours?*). Given today's technology, it usually doesn't matter except for issues of response times and citizen accessibility. For emergency dispatching services, location is less important than it is for fire services, where station location becomes a major issue to addressing response times.

A few years ago, a major fast food company investigated the elimination all of its drive-up window attendants at it restaurants. They had the technology to take a customer's picture at the restaurant in St. Louis and connect it to his/her order, which was taken at a central location in Denver and then sent back to the staff at the St. Louis restaurant. This allowed for orders to be processed faster and with fewer errors (in the fast-food business, speed is the name of the game).

At the experimental stage, the process worked fine—until customers realized they were being photographed. Understandably, they objected, even though the photos were not being saved. The restaurant chain discontinued the project. Lesson learned? Be ready to address unintended consequences.

Modern technology has overcome most of the obstacles that stood in the way of long-standing, common-sense service improvement opportunities. In the 1990s, a county executive in a large county thought it would be more efficient to have one county-wide emergency dispatch center rather than the existing hodge-podge system of small dispatch centers with overlapping services. He felt that one system would not only be more efficient, but that when the costs of all the separate dispatch centers were added together and compared to the cost of one central location, it would be less expensive to all taxpayers. A study proved this point accurate.

The problem arose, however, when discussions focused on which department (turf) would provide the emergency dispatching services. The existing county dispatch center was under the supervision of the county sheriff. In many locations, police chiefs, and to a lesser extent some fire chiefs, tend to not get along well with sheriff departments. This probably stems from the fact that one is elected and the others are appointed.

After much discussion, the county executive convinced the sheriff that dispatching was not one of the sheriff department's core functions. The department's responsibilities focused on operating the jail, traffic patrol and criminal investigations in the more rural areas of the county.

The county dispatching department was separated from the sheriff's department and made into a stand-alone department within the county. A manager was hired to run the dispatch center, and an advisory committee (made up of the sheriff, police chiefs and fire chiefs from throughout the county) was created to develop practical policies and procedures that would work for everyone, as well as address changes as times and needs changed. Not all departments in the county joined the central dispatch center, but most did—and the result has been a service that is better, faster and cheaper.

CHAPTER 6

TECHNOLOGY ISSUES

*"If I had left it to the equine industry to design,
they would have come up with a faster horse!"*
—Henry Ford (on developing the Model T automobile)

Modern technological capabilities have changed the opportunities and enhanced the shared service options for many of the services provided by municipalities. At the same time, technology has also created potential roadblocks to sharing services.

For example, in the field of public safety, enhanced emergency dispatching systems means that dispatchers may know less about the physical features, large buildings and unusual geography of their service areas. Triangulation features of modern emergency communication systems allow dispatchers to identify call locations electronically. This makes it much easier for dispatchers, even from locations outside of the community, to quickly and accurately send emergency equipment and personnel to a caller's location.

In the past, one of the arguments against dispatch consolidation was that dispatchers needed to have extensive knowledge of the community in order to be able to perform their duties effectively and dispatch emergency responders accurately. This is no longer the case in those areas of the country that enjoy enhanced 911 technology in their dispatch centers.

Electronics such as smart phones, wireless laptop computers, and GPS systems make it easier for field operations to share information quickly and accurately. This makes such services as building inspections, property assessing, solid waste collection, public works functions and other activities that require employees to be working in the field to share information efficiently and create additional shared service opportunities.

As technology has made providing municipal services better, faster, and cheaper, it has also made it more complex and has created variations in such things as communications systems, reporting, and recordkeeping due to the many different systems available on the market. There have been many examples of municipalities considering consolidating a department with a neighboring community, only to discover that differences in records management or communications systems are incompatible and extremely expensive to change. It is an argument often raised by department heads who desire to block a consolidation in order to protect their existing turf and municipal kingdom.

When these issues arise, it is important for decision makers to develop long-range operating and capital budgets to determine if these issues are truly obstacles to shared services. In some cases, a current technology nearing the end of its useful life needs to be replaced anyway. This presents a prime opportunity to purchase systems that are compatible with the other interested parties in a shared service discussion. In this case, the department managers and operational staff need to be willing to modify procedures and the way they've "always done things" to be compatible with new technology systems. It is not unusual for upper management to demand process changes in order to make new systems work.

When changing hardware/software and records management systems, it is extremely important to provide adequate funds and time to train all employees expected to utilize the new systems. There are countless examples of new systems not working properly when the root cause was a failure to properly train the employees. This is especially true when a new system is very complex. (Aren't they all these days?)

A classic example of failure to train occurred recently in a municipal finance department of a medium-sized city (population approximately 75,000). The department had a staff of six people, some of whom were already inadequately trained to perform existing financial functions. Including all special funds and utilities, the total budget was nearly $100 million. The city recognized that it needed to upgrade its financial software to handle this growing operation, and a new system was purchased. As part of the acquisition and installation, the software company agreed to provide training to the department employees.

It was then that the finance director failed to do his job. Rather than train all the employees on all the modules of the new software, he only trained some on specific functions. Only the finance director himself was trained on the total software capabilities. This may have been acceptable had the finance director not resigned a few months after installation to take another job. At that point, there was no one who understood the total operation of the financial software—and the city, after hiring a new finance director, spent large and unnecessary sums of money retraining all the employees in the finance department.

When it comes to technology, initial and ongoing training of users and managers is a must!

CHAPTER 7

PERFORMANCE MEASUREMENT

*"If you don't know where you are going,
any road will get you there."*
—Louis Carroll

T he lack of shared project delivery experience in a partnership can make it collapse. To avoid this, it is important to develop and agree upon realistic and measurable service standards at the outset. It is impossible to identify success if there is nothing against which to measure the actions taken or the services provided. Failure to establish measurable standards will likely result in anecdotal information that can doom the effort.

Performance standards lead to a higher level of accountability for management and staff, but there will only be a constructive outcome if the measures are designed to provide incentives and not to deter behavior or punish. Performance measures should be designed to:

- Provide a standard upon which budgets are developed

- Identify and measure the organization's performance
- Provide staff with clear goals to be achieved
- Determine service priorities
- Strive for the achievement of best practices
- Reward, not punish, employees

If performance measures are used to punish employees because they are not meeting standards, they will quickly find ways to develop data that makes them and the department look good. In other words, they will "game" the system (for a further discussion of this phenomenon, see Jonathan Walter's book, *Measuring Up 2.0*).

When it comes to creating measures, many management professionals immediately throw up their hands because they don't know where/how to begin. To help, various types of performance measures to be considered are listed below. Many others can be utilized, but this list can be used to generate ideas to fit an agency's unique needs.

7. PERFORMANCE MEASUREMENT

SERVICE AREA	PERFORMANCE INDICATOR FORMULA
Solid Waste & Refuse	Total cost per dwelling unit (D.U.) collected
	Annual tons of waste per year per residential D.U.
	Cost per ton of garbage collected & land filled
	Number of complaints per 1,000 household collections per year
	Total cost of recycling per D.U.
	Tons of recyclables collected per year per D.U. Cost per ton of recyclables collected Gross cost per ton of recyclables collected Percent of residential waste stream diverted from landfill through curbside recycling (i.e. refuse-to-recycling ratio)
	Net cost per D.U. served per year
	Gross cost per D.U. served per year
Water	1,000 gallons sold per year per capita
	Number of water main breaks per mile of water main Percent of meters tested per year
	Percent of valves exercised per year
	Annual charge per 1,000 gallons
	Complaints per 1,000 customers served
	Percent of unaccounted for water
Wastewater	Percent of gallons treated per gallons of water sold (i.e. infiltration/inflow percentage) Number of manholes repaired/replaced per total number of manholes
	Lineal feet of sanitary sewer jetted per total miles of sanitary sewer
	Permit violations per year
	Charge per 1,000 gallons treated
	Operating cost per 1,000 gallons treated
	Tons of Class A sludge created per 1,000 gallons treated
	Number of sewer backups per mile of sanitary sewer
	Complaints per 1 million gallons served

SERVICE AREA	PERFORMANCE INDICATOR FORMULA
Public Works/ Streets	Overall average street PASER score
	Percent of lane miles rating 5 or higher
	Annual miles of street resurfaced per total miles of substandard (4 or less) street miles
	Lineal feet of sidewalks replaced per total miles of sidewalks
	Lineal feet of storm water sewers jetted/cleaned per total miles of storm sewers
	Number of catch basins repaired/replaced per year per total number of catch basins
	Citizen complaints per 1,000 capita
	Lineal feet of crack sealing per mile of street
	Lane miles swept per year per total miles of street
	Cubic yards of street sweepings collected per lane miles swept
Parks	Street trees planted per 1,000 parcels
	Street trees trimmed per 1,000 parcels
	Tree City USA certification
	Acreage of parkland per 1,000 population
	Cost per acre of parkland
Recreation	Number of youth participants per 1,000 service population
	Number of adult participants per 1,000 service population
	Number of senior participants per 1,000 service population
	Percent of recreation program costs covered by fees
	Total attendance per 1,000 service population

7. PERFORMANCE MEASUREMENT

SERVICE AREA	PERFORMANCE INDICATOR FORMULA
Police	Index crimes/crimes against persons per 1,000 population
	Index crimes/crimes against property per capita
	Average response time (minutes) per call
	Number of telephone calls received by dispatch per capita
	Number of 911 calls per 1,000 capita
	Percent of property recovered to property stolen
	Total complaints/incidents received per 1,000 capita
	Clearance rates Total operating cost per capita
	Total operating cost per sworn FTE officer
Fire/ Rescue	Annual operating fire cost per capita served
	Annual operating EMS cost per capita served
	Annual operating fire & EMS cost per capita served
	Annual loss due to fire per total equalized value of region served
	Average response time (minutes) per call
	Total responses per capita served
	EMS responses per capita
	Fire responses per capita served
	Fire inspection violations per total buildings
	ISO Rating

While the above performance measures are not all-inclusive, this list should assist in initiating discussion among stakeholders to develop the specific needs of a particular shared service effort. However, a word of caution: Most performance measures need time to develop adequate data to be useful. Therefore, ration decisions based on limited data gathered over a short period of time should be avoided, especially if there is an anomaly that occurred during the time of measurement.

When working with performance measures, time and patience are the key ingredients to success. It also takes management and staff to be aware of and develop data that creates true apples-to-apples measurements.

CHAPTER 8

KNOWLEDGE IS KING,
LEADERSHIP IS QUEEN

*"The true sign of intelligence is not knowledge
but imagination."*
—Albert Einstein

In almost every instance of a shared service opportunity, the ultimate decision makers are the local elected officials. These elected officials usually serve their communities on a part-time basis and are far from experts in the operations of the department being considered for consolidation. When it comes to considering a consolidation, they will naturally defer to the organization's "expert," i.e., the impacted department director.

Almost invariably, the department director will advise against the consolidation for the reasons outlined in the chapter on turf protection. Furthermore, most elected officials want to have a positive working relationship with their department directors and often will not try to implement actions in which the director strongly opposes.

This is the key reason shared services have been less successful than one would have anticipated in a period of declining operating revenues. Furthermore, there have been instances where there was not strong political and managerial leadership, which allowed a department director to be able to scuttle a shared service effort.

When a department director opposes a shared service opportunity, there are often mitigating factors that elected officials can take advantage of in order to accomplish a consolidation. One such opportunity may exist when disaster strikes and the situation was not handled particularly well by a department.

CONSTRUCTIVE DISASTERS

Some time ago, a major fire in a small community was beyond the capability of the local fire department to handle. Mutual aid was requested from several neighboring fire departments. In the post-incident evaluation, it was determined that the mutual aid departments lacked compatible communication equipment, different chiefs were giving contradictory orders, and firefighters were confused about how they were to attack the fire. The end result was that a sizable structure burned to the ground.

The elected officials, recognizing that their fire department was not capable of handling large struc-ture fires on their own and that mutual aid had significant flaws, began a study to consider consolidating the area fire departments into a single response entity. The result was a consolidated fire department that was developed out of a "constructive in part because of a disaster." That is, the consolidation would probably not have occurred without having experienced a failed response to a major fire in the community.

POSITION VACANCIES

Another opportunity for a consolidation exists when a department director announces his/her retirement or termination of employment (either voluntarily or involuntarily). In this instance, while the elected officials may no longer have the local "expert" to rely on for counsel and advice, the elected official also does not have the head of a department discounting a shared service opportunity before it might be considered.

Furthermore, with a vacancy in a department, it eliminates one more argument over who will manage consolidated departments. If an organization is considering a consolidation when there is a department director vacancy, the organization can appoint an interim director with no promise of a permanent appointment while a shared service opportunity is studied.

For example, if there are two municipalities considering consolidating their building inspection departments, and the department director in one of the municipalities retires, the argument over which director will be placed in charge of the consolidated department is eliminated (assuming the remaining director is qualified and willing to take over the new department).

POLITICAL TURNOVER

In many cases, timing is everything. There have been many instances when a municipality sees an opportunity to improve service and reduce costs through a collaborative effort, but the opposition of community leadership (perhaps the mayor or council president) greatly influences the decision. When this happens, it may be necessary for the community to bide its time and hope that either the political leader leaves office or that other local leaders can exercise greater influence to move a collaborative effort along.

In the final analysis, it is necessary for decision makers to gain the knowledge they need on a consolidation effort through reliable data that is not one-sided (which may require outside independent assistance). They also may need to be willing to bide their time until the political stars are in alignment in order to achieve their goal of consolidation. This may mean a disaster that could have been handled better, an unacceptable delay in response times, a sudden increase in operating costs or the need to replace expensive capital equipment to mention just a few.

CHAPTER 9

WHO'S IN CHARGE, ANYWAY?

*"Good governance with good intentions
is the hallmark of our government.
Implementation with integrity is our core passion."*
—Narendra Modi

When sharing services with another municipality, the question of who is in charge of the newly formed organization will arise. The immediate answer, of course, is the department director selected to run the newly created department. But in the public sector, the answer is more complex. Those who work in the world of government realize and are accustomed to having an oversight board or committee—usually a group of elected officials (a city council, village board, or county board).

In the case of two or more municipalities forming a shared service arrangement, to whom does the department director report? There are typically two types of organizational structures that provide oversight. One approach is for the department director to report separately to the governing bodies of the municipalities involved in the shared service venture, but this may tax both the time and patience of the director. In this scenario, the director may find himself/herself attending numerous meetings each month and giving reports to and receiving direction from a number of elected bodies. At times, this direction may cause the elected bodies to be at odds. This will quickly frustrate and likely cause any director to begin to seek greener pastures for employment.

A second common arrangement is the creation of a joint oversight board that is made up of representatives from each of the participating municipalities. This group may consist of elected officials, city managers or both. This arrangement means the department director only has one body to report to and take direction from, although agreement between the groups may not always be consistent (often the case with any oversight body).

Creating an effective and sustainable governance structure requires the development of a carefully constructed intergovernmental agreement between the parties. This agreement must be viewed as a win-win arrangement for all of the parties involved. If one or more parties feel taken advantage of by others, or if they do not feel there is equitable treatment among each participant, the deal will fall through.

There are a number of critical elements in an intergovernmental agreement that must be considered and addressed. At a minimum, the elements below should be considered.

REPRESENTATION

If the number of participants in a shared service is an odd number, it is possible to simply have one representative from each municipality serve on the oversight board. If there are five municipalities involved, there might be five members, thus minimizing the potential for tied votes. There are often instances where the municipalities are not of equal size, and the larger community feels that it is paying a greater share of the cost and receiving a greater amount of the service, so it should have a greater number of representatives (i.e., votes) on the oversight board.

Such was the case in a seven-member joint fire department. The communities differed in population, ranging in size from 4,000 to nearly 20,000. Furthermore, some of the municipalities were almost entirely residential, while others had a substantial mix of commercial and industrial representation and required greater service demands.

This group of municipalities essentially took a great leap of faith and decided that even though they had a great deal of diversity, they all had the same goal of providing their communities with a high level of fire and EMS service. They decided to create a governing board that consisted of one representative from each municipality, and this arrangement has worked very well for more than 20 years (although in developing their operating by-laws, they did require a two-thirds vote on capital items, since especially in the fire service, these items can be very expensive).

The presiding chairman in the case above is rotated every two years between the municipalities, which is done in alphabetical order of the municipalities involved. This rotation was more important at the outset so that one municipality was not taking precedence over the other. As time went on, this became unimportant as the municipalities found that they could work well together.

Illustrating the scenario of an equal number of participants, a four-party police agency recently acted on an intergovernmental agreement that created a police board. This board consisted of one representative from each municipality and a fifth member appointed annually by one of the municipalities on a rotating basis. Each year, one municipality would have two votes, but each year who that was would be different. They also required a two-thirds vote to approve expenditures on capital items. This arrangement has also worked very well. Again, it took a bit of a leap of faith of the parties to be willing to put aside parochial interests for the overall good.

TECHNICAL COMMITTEES

While the creation of an effective governing body is of utmost importance, a second concern is that of providing an avenue for management and the rank-and-file employees to share input with organizational operations. After all, the governing body is seldom made up of people with expertise in the service being provided.

A typical solution is to create one or more technical advisory committees. These committees are often a combination of staff employees and management who meet to review policies, procedures and best practices and to make recommendations for changes to the governing body. This is not only important for effective day-to-day operations, but it creates a higher level of buy-in from employees. Such technical committees may be responsible for reviewing and making recommendations on equipment purchases, response policies, activity prioritization, insurance and other benefits issues. Technical committees help demonstrate to employees that management and the governing board care about them and their work and that their input is considered important and valuable.

QUALITY ASSURANCE

Once implementation begins, it almost goes without saying that success is the result of performance. In order to make sure that performance is meeting expectations, management and the governing body must be vigilant in continually monitoring the quality of services being provided. This means insuring that:

- Timelines are being met
- The department is adequately staffed
- Employees are properly trained
- Staff turnover is minimal
- Policies and procedures are always being followed
- The organization remains flexible and able to meet new challenges

This requires a high degree of staff monitoring, which should be done without micro-managing the employees. Management must be directly involved in daily activities and continually monitor weekly, monthly, quarterly and annual data and reports to ensure that work is being done accurately and with minimal errors.

Maintaining a high level of quality in the organization is consistent with developing, monitoring and maintaining the performance measures discussed in Chapter 7. A note of caution, though, in monitoring quality assurance measures: The standards being utilized must be realistic and measurable. Also, management must be sure that employees don't "game the system" or "cook the books." Management's focus here should be on the organization's inputs, activities, outputs and outcomes.

FUNDING CHALLENGES
A critical part of any consolidation is determining how the shared service is going to be financed. This is an important part of any shared service and should be integrated into the intergovernmental agreement.

At the outset of determining how to share the cost of a consolidated department, the over-riding determinant of success and sustainability is that funding must be fair and equitable to all parties. It must treat every participant equally. This does not mean that everyone pays an equal amount toward operating and capital costs. Rather, a funding formula must be used that takes into account the level and frequency of the service being provided. The formula may also be different for operating costs versus capital costs.

A funding formula may include such factors as:

- Population (cost per capita)
- Equalized value (cost per $1000 of value)
- Call volume (cost per 100 calls, tons of waste collected, etc.)
- Types of development being served (residential, commercial, industrial)

- Fixed costs (costs incurred no matter what transpires)

A funding formula may include the above and other factors that fit a specific shared service arrangement. The factors themselves may not all be used or may not all be treated equally. Some may be deemed more important than others or have a greater relationship to costs than others. To accommodate that, the factors can be "weighted." That is, one factor may have a weight of 2 to 3 times that of another. This is not unusual.

There was one fire department consolidation that struggled with how to finance their annual operating costs. As the consolidation agreement was being developed, the consolidation committee considered 15 different funding formulas before it finally found one that was politically acceptable. The agreed-upon formula worked for many years but eventually had to be amended to avoid the organization falling apart. This illustrates how funding methodologies are difficult to create and must have the flexibility to accommodate future changes and conditions.

Often, a consolidated department will be in need of new or additional equipment that is expensive and may require debt financing to acquire. Seldom do these shared service entities have the ability to borrow money—and if they do, it would be at a higher interest rate than that of the typical municipality. Where debt financing is necessary, it is wise to have one of the municipalities serve as the fiscal agent to conduct the borrowing. The intergovernmental agreement will need to have a provision that guarantees the other municipality entities will pay back the fiscal agent.

ASSET DISTRIBUTION

It is common for one or more of the departments that will be joined together to have existing assets that may or may not be useful to the combined department. These assets may be viewed as a "dowry" that each organization is bringing to the "marriage" of the departments—and it can present both challenges and opportunities. In the case of useful assets, it is wise to determine the value of those assets. This may require the need to hire an outside appraiser to determine values. These assets should then be either donated or sold to the new entity.

An alternative to a cash sale is to provide a credit to the selling municipality on future annual operating or capital charges to that municipality. This has been a successful solution in several instances where an immediate cash outlay would have been burdensome to the municipality.

If the assets are not needed by the consolidated department, then the municipality may simply decide to sell those items on the open market in the same manner it uses to dispose of any other surplus property.

IMPLEMENTATION

A strategic implementation plan is necessary to avoid errors and lapses in service. When the "switch" is thrown for the new organization to begin operations, all operating procedures, management structures, equipment and facilities must be in place and ready to function. While there will always be start-up challenges, errors must be kept to an absolute minimum. The critics will be watching for the first opportunity to publicly discredit the new organization if errors occur.

Furthermore, in the public safety arena, there is little room for error as it could very well result in life-threatening situations. To avoid errors or missteps, a period of "off-line" exercises should be conducted and the results assessed, and adjustments and procedural changes should be made prior to actual implementation. The intergovernmental agreement will identify the date for "going live" with the new organization.

DISSOLUTION/EXPANSION PROCESS

What happens if the "marriage" fails? A termination/ withdrawal procedure must be included in the initial intergovernmental agreement and be crystal clear. Most consolidations require investments in capital equipment that may involve long-term debt financing. If one entity decides it no longer wants to be a member of the consolidation, there must be provisions to pay off incurred debt and redistribute assets.

Additionally, if one or more parties decide to terminate their participation, it may likely impact staffing levels. Lengthy notice provisions are necessary to deal with impacts on personnel, budgets, municipal debt and technical procedures. Typically, the termination or removal of a participant is lengthy and difficult.

The parties should have entered into an intergovernmental agreement with a thorough knowledge of service levels, funding and expectations. Once they have committed to this knowledge, the withdrawal process should be lengthy, perhaps as long as three or more years. Typically, this begins with a notice provision and is followed by a cooling-off period to provide an opportunity to either negotiate changes or put future funding and personnel changes in place. The process then may conclude as much as a year later with actual withdrawal.

The creation of a consolidated department may require the investment of substantial capital equipment. This will need to be addressed, as oftentimes additional parties desire to join a consolidation after it is initially created. After all, it would be unfair, for example, if a four-party consolidated emergency dispatch center was created, requiring the purchase of expensive new communications equipment, and a fifth party wanted to join and not contribute toward this investment. The agreement should address how new parties can join the organization and how costs will be reallocated.

Outside assistance from legal counsel, and others who have been involved in creating intergovernmental agreements for other consolidations, is highly recommended.

EPILOGUE

*"Accept the challenges so that you can feel
the exhilaration of victory."*
—George S. Patton

ARE YOU UP TO THE CHALLENGE?

Municipal shared services and consolidations are difficult and complex. They take time and energy to accomplish. As demonstrated in this book, they require skill, leadership, imagination, originality, energy, knowledge, data, perseverance, and a great deal of luck. Governments at all levels are feeling stressed by the lack of sufficient revenues, which is coupled with a reluctance by taxpayers to provide more money through tax increases.

The obvious conclusion, in order to continue to be effective and provide optimal services to its residents, is that governments cannot continue with business as usual. One solution is to consider the consolidation of departments, agencies and whole governmental entities. The private sector has been doing this for years—they just call it mergers and acquisitions, not consolidations and shared services.

The goal of every shared service and consolidation effort is to improve service and save tax dollars. Additionally, these efforts may spur further economic development and streamline processes for the public and a variety of internal and external stakeholders.

To summarize, the necessary ingredients for a successful consolidation include the following components:

- Strong leadership at the top of the organization
- Shared goals by the participants
- Trust between the parties
- Similarity in the culture of the departments, organizations or governments
- A willingness to give up control for the greater good
- Agreements that are win-win for all parties (either in dollars or services)
- Funding systems that are fair and equitable
- Occasionally a constructive disaster
- A good measure of luck

Remember that if this process was easy, everyone would be doing it to save money and improve services. It is a great challenge, but, when successful, it provides immense satisfaction that you have served your taxpayers well by saving them money and improving the services they receive. After all, that is what the goal of every public servant should be.

Some typical examples of shared services and consolidations include:

- Tax Assessing and Property Reevaluations
- Storm Water Maintenance and Compliance
- Health Department / Regionalized Health Services
- Regional Library Systems
- Specialized Training Programs
- County Recycling Programs
- Police and Fire Training Academies and Facilities
- Geographical Information Systems
- Information Technology (IT) Departments
- Consolidated Police Dispatch / 911 Emergency Communications
- Consolidation of Public Work Facilities, Equipment & Departments
- Animal Control / Animal Shelters Facilities
- Records Management / Retention for Municipalities
- Transportation Systems and Routing
- Fleet Maintenance & Purchasing
- Parks and Recreation Facilities, Staff and Maintenance
- Police Department Mergers
- Fire Department Mergers

ACCEPT THE CHALLENGE, GO FORWARD, CONSOLIDATE, AND FEEL THE EXHILARATION OF VICTORY!

ABOUT THE AUTHOR

EDMUND M. HENSCHEL IS semi-retired from over 40 years of municipal management and consulting. As a city manager, he has successfully served four municipalities in two Midwest states.

Currently a municipal consultant, Ed conducts numerous department operation reviews and shared service studies throughout the United States for a range of municipalities from small towns to cities the size of Chicago. He also served as the Executive Director of the Wisconsin City/County Management Association for over 10 years.

Among his many accomplishments, Ed served as one of three negotiators at a bargaining table representing suburban communities against a large regional sewer district that resulted in a settlement of more than $150 million. He was involved in the creation of a fire department consolidation involving seven municipalities. He was selected by his municipal colleagues as President (and later Executive Director) of the Wisconsin City/County Management Association, President of the Milwaukee Area Municipal Employers Association, Chair of the North Shore Public Safety Dispatch Center, and President of Southeast Urban Data Systems.

Ed is currently on the board of directors for a statewide independent public policy think tank organization and serves on a county sheriff's department's disciplinary review committee.

In 2014, he received the prestigious Meritorious Award from the Wisconsin City/County Management Association. In 2015, he received the Lifetime Achievement Award from the Public Policy Forum (now called the Wisconsin Policy Forum), a Wisconsin think tank organization.

Ed continues to be active as a consultant helping municipalities find ways to work better, faster and cheaper. He also is an adjunct professor at the University Wisconsin–Milwaukee, teaching a graduate course in public administration, seeking to help develop the next generation of public administrators.

Ed has published articles on shared services and consolidation in several national and state magazines and made presentations on the topic at numerous professional conferences.

If you would like to contact Ed, you can email him at ehenschel@rwmanagmentgroup.com or henschel.wcma@yahoo.com

CPSIA information can be obtained
at www.ICGtesting.com
Printed in the USA
FSHW022018250519
58398FS